Turning
PRO

Turning
PRO

Tap Your Inner Power and Create Your Life's Work

STEVEN PRESSFIELD

Black Irish Entertainment LLC

NEW YORK   **LOS ANGELES**

BLACK IRISH ENTERTAINMENT LLC
65 CENTRAL PARK WEST
NEW YORK, NY 10023

PORTIONS OF SEVERAL CHAPTERS HAVE APPEARED PREVIOUSLY AS BLOG POSTS
IN THE "WRITING WEDNESDAYS" SERIES FEATURED ON
WWW.STEVENPRESSFIELD.COM

FOR THE GENEROUS PERMISSION TO QUOTE FROM HER WORK,
THE AUTHOR ACKNOWLEDGES THE FOLLOWING SOURCE:

COMPOSED BY ROSANNE CASH © 2010.
REPRODUCED BY PERMSSION FROM VIKING PENGUIN,
A MEMBER OF PENGUIN GROUP (USA) INC.

FIRST BLACK IRISH ENTERTAINMENT PAPERBACK EDITION APRIL 2012

FOR INFORMATION ABOUT SPECIAL DISCOUNTS OR BULK PURCHASES,
PLEASE VISIT WWW.BLACKIRISHBOOKS.COM OR WWW.STEVENPRESSFIELD.COM

ISBN: 978-1-936891-03-0

PRINTED IN THE UNITED STATES OF AMERICA
1 2 3 4 5 6 7 8 9 10

for

KATE SNOW

I wrote in *The War of Art* that I could divide my life neatly into two parts: before turning pro and after. After is better.

— Steven Pressfield

FOREWORD

by Shawn Coyne

After editing his novels *Gates of Fire*, *Tides of War*, and *Last of the Amazons*, I published Steven Pressfield's first nonfiction work, *The War of Art*. When I presented the book to the sales representatives—I was running a boutique publishing company called Rugged Land Books at the time—I suggested that this lean, take-no-prisoners document would become an evergreen backlist bestseller. It's now ten years later and, with hundreds of thousands of copies sold, Steve's book is an in-the-studio, on-the-bedside-table, must-have inspirational reference for working artists everywhere.

Have you ever taken a good look at a public garbage can in Paris, a paving stone in Rio de Janeiro, or a doorway in Dublin? Trust me—the man or woman responsible for making those utilitarian objects was creating art. When craft, dedication, and professionalism come together, the result can be astonishing. Sometimes the work even achieves immortality.

But sitting down to do the work is another thing entirely. Call it writer's block, artistic *agita*, or general malaise, that malignant internal entity that keeps us from our calling can be a killer. Painting, writing, starting a new business venture, doing charity work, or even just putting everything we have into the work we're already doing is waylaid again and again by that chattering critic inside our heads.

In *The War of Art,* Steve gave a name to this voice. He called it Resistance. Resistance stops us from committing to the important work of our lives—not just committing to it, but fighting like hell to get it done.

What to do?

The War of Art suggests a strategy to bring the fight to this perverse enemy. Steve calls it "turning pro." When we turn pro, we leave our amateur ways behind and announce, if only within ourselves, that we have earned our battle scars and learned from our wayward ways to brand ourselves as professionals.

Over the past ten years, Steve has been asked again and again,"How exactly do you turn pro?" What does turning pro really mean? What do professionals do that the rest of us don't?

Steve worked for three years on *Turning Pro.* His goal was to try to find a deeper and, at the same time, more practical approach to making the transition from amateur to professional. This approach took so long to materialize that he published two other nonfiction books—*The Warrior Ethos* and *Do the Work* (with Seth Godin's Domino Project)—waiting for this one to come together. It was too important to be rushed. I think you'll be glad that the wait is over.

You'll notice, on the spine of this book (or in the title page of your eBook), that the company publishing *Turning Pro* is called Black Irish Books. It is my great pleasure to declare that Black Irish Books is just another name for two guys (Steve and I) who battle Resistance every single day...just as you do.

It's no secret that book publishing is in the midst of radical change. The barriers to entry have crumbled and, as a result, opportunities have grown exponentially. Steve and I joined forces as co-founders of Black Irish Books to get into the ring ourselves.

We intend to publish steak-and-potato kind of books whose aim is to inspire, encourage, and fortify those artists, entrepreneurs, and athletes whose ambition is not to stand on the sidelines, waiting for permission from others, but to take their destiny in their own fists—to pursue their heart's calling and make it work.

Turning Pro is not just something we're publishing. We're living it, too.

BOOK ONE

THE AMATEUR LIFE

THE HUMAN CONDITION

The Daily Show reported recently that scientists in Japan had invented a robot that is capable of recognizing its own reflection in a mirror.

"When the robot learns to hate what it sees," said Jon Stewart, "it will have achieved full humanity."

THREE MODELS OF
SELF-TRANSFORMATION

W hen we hate our lives and ourselves, two models present themselves as modes of salvation.

The first is the therapeutic model. In the therapeutic model, we are told (or we tell ourselves) that we are "sick." What ails us is a "condition" or a "disease."

A condition or a disease may be remedied by "treatment."

Right now we are "ill." After treatment, we will be "well." Then we will be happy and will be able to function productively in society and in the world.

That's one way of looking at our troubles.

The second way is the moralistic model. The moralistic model is about good and evil. The reason we are unhappy, we are told (or tell ourselves) is that we have done something "wrong." We have committed a "crime" or a "sin."

In some versions of the moralistic model, we don't even have to have done anything wrong. The human being, we are told, was born wrong.

The answer to the condition of wrongness is punishment and penance. When we have "served our sentence" and "atoned for our sins," we will be "pardoned" and "released."

Then we will be happy and will be able to function productively in society and in the world.

This book proposes a third model.

The model this book proposes is the model of the amateur and the professional.

The thesis of this book is that what ails you and me has nothing to do with being sick or being wrong. What ails us is that we are living our lives as amateurs.

The solution, this book suggests, is that we turn pro.

Turning pro is free, but it's not easy. You don't need to take a course or buy a product. All you have to do is change your mind.

Turning pro is free, but it's not without cost. When we turn pro, we give up a life with which we may have become extremely comfortable. We give up a self that we have come to identify with and to call our own. We may have to give up friends, lovers, even spouses.

Turning pro is free, but it demands sacrifice. The passage is often accompanied by an interior odyssey whose trials are survived only at great cost, emotionally, psychologically, and spiritually. We pass through a membrane when we turn pro. It hurts. It's messy and it's scary. We tread in blood when we turn pro.

Turning pro is not for everyone. We have to be a little crazy to do it, or even to want to. In many ways the passage chooses us; we don't choose it. We simply have no alternative.

What we get when we turn pro is, we find our power. We find our will and our voice and we find our self-respect. We become who we always were but had, until then, been afraid to embrace and to live out.

Do you remember where you were on 9/11? You'll remember where you were when you turn pro.

MY LIFE AS AN AMATEUR

When I was in my twenties, I lived for a winter in a boarding house in Durham, North Carolina that served as a halfway station for patients emerging from state mental hospitals. I wasn't a mental patient myself, but the law of metaphor had brought me to this place as surely as if I had been.

The people in the halfway house were by no means "crazy." They were as interesting and complex a collection of individuals as I had ever met. I made friends. I found a home.

We did a lot of talking in the evenings in the halfway house. We gathered over coffee in the communal kitchen and talked about books and politics and whether aliens were messengers from the future or from God.

I was the only one in the halfway house who had a job. I was making $1.75 an hour in the body shop of a trucking company, training to become an over-the-road trucker. Everyone else in the halfway house got a check from the state. Social workers appeared from time to time to evaluate the people in the halfway house, to check on their progress, and to counsel them in their re-integration into society and the real world.

I began to wonder how I came to be in this house with these people. Why did I feel so at home? Was this my destiny?

Then one night I had a dream. In the dream I came into my room and found that my shirts had all folded themselves in the drawer (instead of being mashed together in their usual jumbled mess). My boots had crawled out from under the bed where I normally kicked them when I took them off and had set themselves upright and tidy. They had shined themselves.

When I woke up, I thought, "I'm ambitious! I have ambition!"

I didn't tell anyone in the halfway house about the dream. In fact I haven't told anyone to this day. I kept the dream private. It was my secret.

It took me a long time to come to terms with the idea that I had ambition. I felt guilty about it. Who was I to aspire to "rise above" my brothers and sisters or to aim to be "better" than anybody else?

In the halfway house, the dominant emotion was fear. No one ever spoke of it, but fear pervaded every centimeter of that space. Everyone in the house had, in his or her own way, experienced the disintegration of their personality. Everyone had fallen a long way, fallen hard, and fallen alone. Everyone in that house had looked their own annihilation in the face, and it had scared the hell out of them.

I decided that I had to leave the halfway house. I found a cinderblock cabin along a highway in the country that rented for fifteen dollars a week. I still have a photo of that house. The house had no electricity, no toilet, no running water, and no heat. It had a front door but no back door. There were no windows and no furniture. I slept on a mattress that I pushed into a corner where the rain couldn't reach it. I cooked my meals outdoors in back, over a fire of pine kindling that I collected from the woods.

I had started driving for the trucking company by then. I was being assigned my first loads and sent out on the road for the first time, so it didn't matter too much where I called home. Most nights I slept in the truck's sleeper berth. I ate my meals in cafés and truck stops on the road.

The reason I keep a photo of that house is that it changed my life. To find that house and to move into it was my first act, as an adult, that embraced the idea of ambition.

Ambition, I have come to believe, is the most primal and sacred fundament of our being. To feel ambition and to act upon it is to embrace the unique calling of our souls. Not to act upon that ambition is to turn our backs on ourselves and on the reason for our existence.

Those first stirrings of ambition saved me and put me on the path to becoming an artist and a professional.

MY FIRST HERO

There was a redheaded cat who used to come around sometimes when I lived in that house in the country. He was a battle-scarred old tom who lived in the woods. On nights when I was home, I would cook supper over a little fire out back. The cat would materialize and sit across from me while I ate. I tried to toss him scraps of meat from time to time, but he wouldn't take them. He was nobody's pet.

The geography of our dinners together was that I would sit on the cinderblock step at the back of the house. The fire was in front of me inside a circle of stones on a patch of grass. The woods started ten feet away. The redheaded cat would sit at the edge of the woods, facing me. He didn't lie down. He sat up, facing me, with his big front paws beneath him.

The cat regarded me with an expression that was somewhere between condescension and disdain. There was no doubt in either of our minds which one of us was the superior being or which one possessed self-command and self-sovereignty. There was no doubt which one could take care of himself and which one had his shit together. That cat looked at me as if he was trying to decide whether or not to kick my ass.

I admired that redheaded cat. He became a role model for me. I wanted to be like that redheaded cat. I missed him when he didn't come around.

I regarded the apparition of that redheaded cat as a good omen and a sign that, maybe, I was on the right path.

MY SMITH-CORONA

What was really happening in that house in the country?

What was happening was I was hiding.

In the back of my Chevy van, under piles of junk and rusting spare parts, sat my ancient Smith-Corona typewriter. Why didn't I throw it away? I certainly wasn't using it.

Fear and shame hung over me and over that house, just as they permeated every crack and cranny of the halfway house back in town. I was terrified of sitting down at that Smith-Corona and trying to write something, and ashamed of myself because I knew I was terrified, but I was still too scared to act.

My ambition was to write, but I had buried it so deep that it only peeked out in dreams and moments of insight that appeared at odd instants and then vanished without a trace.

Everything I was doing in my outer life was a consequence and an expression of that terror and that shame.

SHADOW CAREERS

Sometimes, when we're terrified of embracing our true calling, we'll pursue a shadow calling instead. That shadow career is a metaphor for our real career. Its shape is similar, its contours feel tantalizingly the same. But a shadow career entails no real risk. If we fail at a shadow career, the consequences are meaningless to us.

Are you pursuing a shadow career?

Are you getting your Ph.D. in Elizabethan studies because you're afraid to write the tragedies and comedies that you know you have inside you? Are you living the drugs-and-booze half of the musician's life, without actually writing the music? Are you working in a support capacity for an innovator because you're afraid to risk becoming an innovator yourself?

If you're dissatisfied with your current life, ask yourself what your current life is a metaphor for.

That metaphor will point you toward your true calling.

MY SHADOW CAREER

My shadow career (I've had more than one) was driving tractor-trailers.

In my late twenties and early thirties, I drove trucks for a living. I drove up and down the East Coast out of Durham, North Carolina, and later cross-country, based out of Seaside, California. I was in deadly earnest and committed 100% to making my life as an over-the-road trucker.

What I was really doing was running away from writing.

Driving trucks was for me a shadow version of writing, because being a truck driver was, in my imagination, powerful and manly (just as I imagined being a writer would be). It was interesting; it was never boring. It was a career I could take pride in, an occupation that felt right to me.

Driving trucks was honest labor. You worked for a dollar and you got paid a dollar. The men I drove with were salt-of-the-earth, stand-up guys, just as I aspired to be. And it took courage to be a trucker. Rolling over the mountains at night from western Carolina and Virginia into West Virginia was serious business. Wicked uphills followed drop-dead downhills, around breakneck curves, most of them unlighted and unmarked, so that in order to carry speed into the next uphill (which you had to do, or the ascending grade would drop you down into creeper gear, with every other trucker on the mountain piling up behind you, cursing), you had to keep your right foot nailed to the floor while letting 60,000 pounds of truck and load plunge you downhill as fast as they could.

Then there was the romance of "the road." I loved the road because it always took you somewhere. You were never stuck in one place. Delivering a load to a factory or a warehouse, I could hang with the locals and shoot the breeze—but I always knew that, while they were trapped, I was free. In a few minutes I'd be clear of town and rolling down the highway.

Of course this was all self-delusion.

The road was taking me nowhere.

I wasn't writing books. I wasn't facing my demons. I was spectating at life through the movie screen of a cab-over windshield, while every mile I traveled only carried me farther away from where I needed to go and from who I needed to become.

THREE CHEERS FOR THE
AMATEUR LIFE

B efore we begin ruthlessly deconstructing the amateur life, let's pause for a moment to give it its due. The amateur life is our youth. It's our hero's journey.

No one is born a pro. You've got to fall before you hit bottom, and sometimes that fall can be a hell of a ride.

So here's to blackouts and divorces, to lost jobs and lost cash and lost self-respect. Here's to time on the street. Here's to years we can't remember. Here's to bad friends and cheating spouses—and to us, too, for being guilty of both.

Becoming a pro, in the end, is nothing grander than growing up.

What exactly are shadow careers? What is the amateur life? What are addictions and obsessions and displacement activities? How can we learn from them, and profit from them, when we finally put our days on the street behind us and begin to live our real lives?

MY SHADOW CAREER. PART TWO

When I was in high school, I read a book by Jack Kerouac called *On The Road*. The book blew my brains out. The "beat," bohemian life that Kerouac described was, I thought, the coolest, most romantic thing I had ever heard of. I loved the idea of traveling around the country, working jobs and meeting people and submerging yourself in "real life."

A lot of other kids read that book and thought the same thing. But very few were dumb enough to actually try to live it.

Again, I was getting the writer's life confused with real life.

My trucking career was an attempt to professionalize a life on the road. It was not a bad idea, actually. It beat the hell out of my prior years of aimlessly drifting from East Coast to West and north to south, wondering why the life I was living wasn't measuring up to the cool, beat times that Jack Kerouac had found.

But life is strange, and things work out in their own weird way.

When I finally did turn pro and started getting books published, my literary agent turned out to be a gentleman named Sterling Lord of Sterling Lord Literistic, in New York. Sterling had represented Jack Kerouac. It was Sterling who made the original publishing deal for *On The Road*.

THE SHADOW LIFE

In the shadow life, we live in denial and we act by addiction. We pursue callings that take us nowhere and permit ourselves to be controlled by compulsions that we cannot understand (or are not aware of) and whose outcomes serve only to keep us caged, unconscious and going nowhere.

The shadow life is the life of the amateur. In the shadow life we pursue false objects and act upon inverted ambitions.

The shadow life, the life of the amateur and the addict, is not benign.

The longer we cleave to this life, the farther we drift from our true purpose, and the harder it becomes for us to rally the courage to get back.

ADDICTED TO LOVE

I have a friend who's addicted to love. (I can relate to this addiction myself.) I've known her my whole life, and it's absolutely excruciating to listen to the chronicle of her romances. She migrates from one passionate, all-consuming affair to the next. She is in agony throughout the affair, and the affair always ends in agony. It will not surprise you, I'm sure, when I report that this woman is one of the most gifted, talented people I've ever met. She's a piano prodigy. Her photographs win prizes. And she's a near-world-class athlete; she has swum the Maui-Big Island open-ocean crossing half a dozen times.

Over the years, my friend has developed a philosophy—you could almost call it a religion—about pursuing the sublime through love. This philosophy is so complex and so convincing that she can not only persuade herself of its reality, but you or me too if we sit still long enough to listen to her. She is mesmerizing. At the same time, the experience is bone-numbingly tedious, watching her transit from one great love to the next, with each drama playing out to exactly the same cadence, and each one culminating in exactly the same dead end.

My friend knows this is Resistance. We've talked about it a hundred times. She's running away from her gifts and she knows it. But the habit is too strong. She has become identified with it. It's who she is.

HABITS

This book is about habits.

The difference between an amateur and a professional is in their habits. An amateur has amateur habits. A professional has professional habits.

We can never free ourselves from habits. The human being is a creature of habit. But we can replace bad habits with good ones. We can trade in the habits of the amateur and the addict for the practice of the professional and the committed artist or entrepreneur.

It may help, as a jumping-off place, to consider the interior world of the most passionate and tragic creature of habit—the addict.

BEAUTIFUL LOSERS

Have you ever noticed that addicts are often extremely interesting people?

Addiction itself is excruciatingly boring. It's boring because it's predictable—the lies, the evasions, the transparent self-justifications and self-exonerations. But the addict himself is often a colorful and fascinating person.

If he has been a substance abuser for any length of time, his story often reads like a novel, packed with drama, conflict, and intrigue. If the addict's drug of choice is alcohol, the narrative is frequently one of job loss, domestic abuse, divorce, abandonment of children, bankruptcy. If Class One narcotics are the culprit, the tale often includes troubles with the law, crime, prison time, violence, even death.

Of course, you and I can be addicted to any number of things—to love, to sex, to worship of our children or our parents, to dominance, to submission. We can even be addicted to ourselves (see Charlie Sheen, Donald Trump). Such individuals can be absolutely fascinating at the same time that they're boring as hell.

What, then, is the connection between addiction and Resistance?

ART AND ADDICTION

For the past several years, I've written a weekly post on my website (www.stevenpressfield.com) called "Writing Wednesdays." Far and away, the most popular entries in that space have been in my "Artist and Addict" series. One of the points those posts made was that there's not that big a difference between an artist and an addict.

Many artists are addicts, and vice versa. Many are artists in one breath and addicts in another.

What's the difference?

The addict is the amateur; the artist is the professional.

Both addict and artist are dealing with the same material, which is the pain of being human and the struggle against self-sabotage. But the addict/amateur and the artist/professional deal with these elements in fundamentally different ways.

(When I say "addiction," by the way, I'm not referring only to the serious, clinical maladies of alcoholism, drug dependence, domestic abuse and so forth. Web-surfing counts too. So do compulsive texting, sexting, twittering and Facebooking.)

Distractions.

Displacement activities.

When we're living as amateurs, we're running away from our calling—meaning our work, our destiny, the obligation to become our truest and highest selves.

Addiction becomes a surrogate for our calling. We enact the addiction instead of embracing the calling. Why? Because to follow a calling requires work. It's hard. It hurts. It demands entering the pain-zone of effort, risk, and exposure.

So we take the amateur route instead. Instead of composing our symphony, we create a "shadow symphony," of which we ourselves are the orchestra, the conductor, the composer, and the audience. Our life becomes a shadow drama, a shadow start-up company, a shadow philanthropic venture.

Have you ever been to New Orleans? In Tennessee Williams-esque Southern cities (Savannah and Charleston also come to mind), you find "characters." The colorful old lady with 39 cats, the purple-haired dude who has turned his apartment into a shrine to James Dean. In the South you can get away with that stuff. It's kinda cool. The shadow enactment has been elevated to such a level that it becomes folklore, even (almost) art.

My life used to be a shadow novel. It had plot, characters, sex scenes, action scenes. It had mood, atmosphere, texture. It was scary, it was weird, it was exciting. I had friends who were living out shadow movies, or creating shadow art, or initiating shadow industries. These were our addictions, and we worked them for all they were worth. There was only one problem: none of us was writing a real novel, or painting a real painting, or starting a real business. We were amateurs living in the past or dreaming of the future, while failing utterly to do the work necessary to progress in the present.

When you turn pro, your life gets very simple.

The Zen monk, the artist, the entrepreneur often lead lives so plain they're practically invisible. Miyamoto Musashi's dojo was smaller than my living room. Things became superfluous for him. In the end he didn't even need a sword.

The amateur is an egotist. He takes the material of his personal pain and uses it to draw attention to himself. He creates a "life," a "character," a "personality."

The artist and the professional, on the other hand, have turned a corner in their minds. They have succeeded in stepping back from themselves. They have grown so bored with themselves and so sick of their petty bullshit that they can manipulate those elements the way a HazMat technician handles weapons-grade plutonium.

They manipulate them for the good of others. What were once their shadow symphonies become real symphonies. The color and drama that were once outside now move inside.

Turning pro is an act of self-abnegation. Not Self with a capital-S, but little-s self. Ego. Distraction. Displacement. Addiction.

When we turn pro, the energy that once went into the Shadow Novel goes into the real novel. What we once thought was real—"the world," including its epicenter, ourselves—turns out to be only a shadow. And what had seemed to be only a dream becomes, now, the reality of our lives.

RESISTANCE AND ADDICTION

The pre-addictive individual—i.e., you and I when we're young—experiences a calling. To art, to service, to honorable sacrifice. In other words, we experience positive aspiration. A vision of the higher, realized self we might become.

The intimation of this calling is followed immediately by the apparition of Resistance.

Fear.

Self-doubt.

Self-sabotage.

What makes this moment so soul-precarious is that most of us are unconscious, in the event, of both our aspirations and our Resistance. We're asleep. We know only that something is wrong and we don't know how to fix it. We're restless. We're bored. We're angry. We burn to accomplish something great, but we don't know where to begin and, even if we did, we'd be so terrified that we still couldn't take a step.

Enter: a drink, a lover, a habit.

Addiction replaces aspiration.

The quick fix wins out over the long, slow haul.

ADDICTION AND SHADOW CAREERS

When we can't stand the fear, the shame, and the self-reproach that we feel, we obliterate it with an addiction.

The addiction becomes the shadow version, the evil twin of our calling to service or to art.

That's why addicts are so interesting and so boring at the same time.

They're interesting because they're called to *something*—something new, something unique, something that we, watching, can't wait to see them bring forth into manifestation.

At the same time, they're boring because they never do the work.

Instead, the addict enacts his aspiration in shadow form. The addiction becomes his novel, his adventure, his great love. The work of art or service that might have been produced is replaced by the drama, conflict, and suffering of the addict's crazy, haunted, shattered life.

THE ADDICT AS DRAMATIC HERO

Robert McKee, in his story seminars, testifies that the essential quality in a fictional protagonist—i.e., the hero in a book or a movie—is that he or she must possess the passion and the will to push the story to the limits of human experience in order to achieve their goal.

(Otherwise there would be no story.)

This heroic monomania is also the definition of the addict. The lush or the junkie will sell her own mother to score the substance she is jonesing for.

WHY I DON'T KNOCK ADDICTION

A ddictions are not "bad." They are simply the shadow forms of a more noble and exalted calling. Our addictions are our callings themselves, only encrypted and incognito.

They are a metaphor for our best selves, the coded version of our higher aspirations.

Addictions and shadow careers are messages in a bottle from our unconscious. Our Self, in the Jungian sense, is trying to get our attention, to have an intervention with us.

The question we need to ask of a shadow career or an addiction is the same question the psychotherapist asks of a dream. "What is our unconscious trying to tell us?"

PULLING THE PIN

When I was twenty-nine, I spent a season picking apples in Chelan, Washington. The job sounds idyllic, I know, but it was hard, hard work. It was migrant labor.

The season lasted six weeks. It started with the Romes, then moved on to the Deliciouses; when the cold started, the Winesaps came in. These were the hardest to pick. They cut the flesh of your hands with their sharp, barbed spurs, particularly when you picked them before the sun came up, with frost on the stems and your fingers frozen. One of the top pickers was a guy named Dave, who had been an infantryman with the 1st Marine Division at the Chosin Reservoir in Korea, November-December 1950, when temperatures fell to thirty below zero and the beleagured American troops were surrounded by 67,000 soldiers of the Chinese Ninth Army—one of the most hellish and valiant ordeals in U.S. military history. I asked Dave how he picked Winesaps. "With a great deal of pain," he said.

Dave was a terrific guy—smart, funny, kind and generous—who had chosen to live "on the fritz," as the Wobblies used to say back in the Twenties. He was a drinker who lived most of the year in an SRO hotel on Skid Row in Seattle (the term "Skid Row," Dave told me, derived from the original "Skid Road" in Seattle, where the lumbermen used to slide their timber to the harbor on skids), but he came out on the tramp at harvest time to work the apples in Washington and the cherries in Marysville, California. Dave got a veteran's disability check from Uncle Sam, but he was such a good picker that he could put away a nice wad of cash for winter with a few months' labor in the fall.

You get paid by the bin (4' by 4' by 3' deep) for picking apples. I could do two a day when I started, never more than three. Dave routinely knocked off six, seven, eight. We got $4 a bin, maybe six; I can't remember. There was also a dollar-a-bin bonus at the end of the season if you stuck around.

Dave stuck, and so did I. Most of the tramps "pulled the pin."

What is a tramp anyway? Dave explained: "A tramp is an itinerant worker. A hobo is an itinerant non-worker. A bum is a non-itinerant non-worker."

The term "pulling the pin" comes from the old days of riding the rails. To uncouple one car from another, the train crew pulled a heavy steel pin out of the coupling mechanism.

In migrant lingo, pulling the pin meant quitting. You'd wake up and the bunk next to you would be empty. "What happened to Jim?" "He pulled the pin."

I could relate to pulling the pin. I pulled the pin on my first book, 99.9% of the way through. I pulled the pin on my marriage. I had never done anything in my life to that point where I hadn't pulled the pin.

I was determined, now, NOT to pull the pin.

I asked Dave why he and the other tramps drank wine.

"Hard liquor will destroy your liver," he said. "Good whisky is expensive and the cheap stuff is poison. Beer? You have to drink a case minimum to get where you need to get. If you don't have a car, how can you carry it? Plus, you're pissing all night long. Wine is best. You can get a decent buzz on a bottle or two, and the stuff is made, at least partly, from a natural product—grapes. Who knows, there might even be a tad of nutrition in there."

I was the only person in the bunkhouse who had a vehicle, so I gave everybody rides into town. Mostly they stayed on the orchard though. Work started at first light; by the end of the day, most of the men were so tired they just wanted to kill a bottle or two and snug down under a blanket.

I didn't drink. Instead I talked to everybody.

Jack was probably the coolest of the "fruit tramps." He looked like Steve McQueen and was an ace car mechanic, as well as being almost as fast a picker as Dave. He used to cough up blood in such quantities that his pillow couldn't be laundered; they had to throw it away. I asked Jack why he didn't get a real job. He was going to kill himself, it was clear, if he stayed out on the road.

"I tried, man, many times. Last year my sister's husband took me in, back in Enid, Oklahoma, where I'm from. Had a job, nice little apartment, even had a girlfriend."

I asked him what happened.

"One morning I woke up, just couldn't take it no more. Pulled the pin."

PULLING THE PIN, PART TWO

Two things struck me about the migrants in that bunkhouse. First, they were wonderful guys. There weren't crazy, they weren't stupid. They would teach you and help you; they'd share anything, down to their last dollar. They were funny and smart. Many of them were readers; a good portion kept up with politics and had more insight to contribute than the paid pundits on the airwaves.

Second, they had achieved the kind of peace that comes when you've already fallen so far that you don't have to worry about falling any farther. Worse come to worst, Dave or Jack could have slept on the ground, foraged for grub. If the Bomb went off tomorrow, they'd survive just fine.

There was something very natural, I thought, about a life following the seasons. The human race did that for millions of years. When the season finished in Washington, the next crop was coming into harvest down in California. "You coming for the cherries?" Dave asked me.

I wanted to. If I hadn't had a book I had to finish (so I could stop pulling the pin) and my cat, Mo, to look after, I'd've done it. I gave Dave a ride out to the highway. I could see him in my rearview, with his thumb out, heading south as I was going west.

The life we call "normal" isn't normal at all. A spouse and kids, a mortgage, a 9-to-5 job...who said that was life? What's so great about working in a factory or a cubicle?

You and I, who are artists and entrepreneurs, live a life that's closer to natural, if you ask me.

We migrate, too. We follow the Muse instead of the sun. When one crop is picked, we hit the road and move on to the next.

It's a not a bad life.

It's lonely. It's tough. It ain't for everyone. But, like the life of a migrant on the road, it has its compensations.

Dave may have been a drinker (and he certainly wasn't going to quit), but that was the life he had chosen. Would his mother and father, his sisters and his ex-wife, have picked this kind of life for him? Would he himself have elected it?

But Dave was willing to pay the price for the choices he had made. He paid it in hard work and hard times and the looks people gave him when they passed him on the street.

They didn't know Dave.

He was a top hand and a good guy. He would never pull the pin.

He was a pro.

THE DEFINITION OF BORING

Something that's boring goes nowhere. It travels in a circle. It never arrives at its destination.

The repetitive nature of the shadow life and of addiction is what makes both so tedious. No traction is ever gained. No progress is made. We're stuck in the same endlessly-repeating loop.

That's what makes addiction like hell.

All addictions share, among others, two primary qualities.

1. They embody repetition without progress.

2. They produce incapacity as a payoff.

THE PAYOFF OF INCAPACITY

Remember my friend who is addicted to love?

She's charming, she's interesting, she's beautiful and adventurous and intelligent. If you saw a story about her in *Vanity Fair*, you might think, "Wow, what a brilliant life this woman leads, full of drama and romance and glamour! I wish I had that life."

I love my friend, but she has wasted her life.

I know because I've wasted vast tracts of my own.

My friend has used the pursuit of love to produce incapacity, and it has worked for her for decades. Her multiple talents have gone unexplored, untried, and unrealized. She has become a version of herself, but it is a shadow version, an inverted version, a crippled version. She is miserable and she cannot, or will not, change.

You might disagree with me. You might say my friend has a great life. You might be right.

Distraction and displacement seem innocent on the surface. How can we be harming ourselves by having fun, or seeking romance, or enjoying the fruits of this big, beautiful world?

But lives go down the tubes one repetition at a time, one deflection at a time, one hundred and forty characters at a time.

The following is a sampling, in no particular order, of garden-variety addictions that fall short of hard-core chemical dependency but are still more than potent enough to cripple, malform, and destroy our lives.

ADDICTED TO FAILURE

There's a difference between failing (which is a natural and normal part of life) and being addicted to failure. When we're addicted to failure, we enjoy it. Each time we fail, we are secretly relieved.

There's a glamour to failure that has been mined for centuries by starving poets, romantic suicides, and other self-defined doomed souls. This glamour inverts failure and turns it into "success."

I've had a romance with this goddess myself. Have you? The lure of failure can be as intoxicating as the hardest of hard-core narcotics.

Its payoff is incapacity. When we fail, we are off the hook. We have given ourselves a Get Out Of Jail Free card. We no longer have to ask and answer Stanislavsky's famous three questions:

Who am I? Why am I here? What do I want?

ADDICTED TO SEX

If addictions and shadow careers are metaphors, sex is the richest one of all and the most difficult to decode.

Why are we obsessed with sex? Does sex represent conquest or surrender? Are we seeking the oblivion of orgasm or the transcendence of escaping the ego?

Is union with another our goal, or are we seeking to dominate or humiliate our partner?

Is sex about love? Are we seeking a soul-mate, a mother/father? Are we trying to reach God?

"I don't see what all the fuss about sex is," said the comedian. "It's only friction."

My own theory is that the obsessive pursuit of sex is an attempt to obliterate the ego, i.e., "normal" consciousness, the monkey-mind that tortures us with restlessness, fear, anger, and self-centeredness.

We're trying to get to the level above that.

The entity we're seeking union with is ourselves.

We're trying to connect with our true being, our soul, our Self.

ADDICTED TO DISTRACTION

Resistance hates two qualities above all others: concentration and depth. Why? Because when we work with focus and we work deep, we succeed.

How did Tom Brady master the art of the forward pass? How did Picasso paint? How did Yo-Yo Ma learn the cello?

Resistance wants to keep us shallow and unfocused. So it makes the superficial and the vain intoxicating.

Have you checked your e-mail in the last half hour? When you sit down to do your work, do you leave your web connection on?

It can be fatal, keeping up with the Kardashians.

ADDICTED TO MONEY

The real utility of money is its convenience as a medium of exchange. If you and I have a goat in Smyrna, we don't have to carry the poor beast in our arms all the way to Aleppo to trade it for a carpet. We can sell the goat in Smyrna, stash a silver daric in our pocket, then take the daric to Aleppo to buy the carpet.

But when we're addicted to money, we become hooked on the metaphor.

Is money how we keep score? Is it magic? Is wealth a currency that opens doors, realizes possibilities, produces transcendence?

Money is second only to sex in the richness of its metaphor. But, as in the case of carnality, our real object is the currency of our own hearts. (The same premise applies to power, fame, and all other external expressions of potency.)

What you and I are really seeking is our own voice, our own truth, our own authenticity.

ADDICTED TO TROUBLE

There are more than two million people behind bars in the United States and another 5M on probation or parole. How many millions more are self-imprisoned in cycles of abuse (of others or of themselves) or habituated to other forms of vice, corruption, and depravity?

Why is trouble so intoxicating?

Because its payoff is incapacity.

The scars and tattoos of the convict are his shadow symphony, his displaced epic, his unpainted masterpiece. The individual addicted to trouble will never get out of jail, because he is safer behind bars than free out in the world. Each time he is released, he will find a way to get sent back.

The payoff for the prisoner is release from the agonizing imperative of identifying, embracing and bringing into material existence the dreams and visions of his own deepest, noblest, and most honorable heart.

MY YEAR OF TURNING PRO

I was 31. I had saved up $2,700 and moved from New York City to a little town in northern California. I rented a house behind another house for $105 a month. I had my old Chevy van, my Smith-Corona typewriter, and my cat, Mo.

Every Monday morning I walked into the village to the Bank of America and took out $25. That sum lasted me for the next seven days.

I didn't talk to anybody during my year of turning pro. I didn't hang out. I just worked. I had a book in mind and I had decided I would finish it or kill myself. I could not run away again, or let people down again, or let myself down again. This was it, do or die.

I had no TV, no radio, no music. No sex, no sports. I didn't read the newspaper. For breakfast I had liver and eggs. I was like Rocky.

In the early mornings, I'd walk down River Road to my friend Paul Rink's house, which was actually a camper-shell mounted on a pickup. Paul was a writer. He had been a friend of Henry Miller's in Big Sur. Paul taught me what books to read and what writers to pay attention to. That was what I did at night. I read all the stuff that you're supposed to read in college but never do, or if you do, you're not paying attention. I read Tolstoy and Dostoevsky and Turgenev. I read Cervantes and Flaubert and Stendhal and Knut Hamsun, and I read every American except Faulkner.

I was writing on my ancient Smith-Corona, which had a heavy carriage that physically shuttled back and forth as I typed. My cat Mo would curl up on the desk, on the left side of the typewriter, so that the carriage would pass over his head, back and forth as I typed. He didn't seem to mind.

When I ran out of money at the end of my time, I went to pick apples in Washington State. That was when I met Dave and Jack. When the season was over, I had cleared two hundred and fifty bucks after paying rent, gas, and engine repairs. I drove south and got back to work on the book.

One day, I typed THE END. That's the moment in *The War of Art* when I knew I had beaten Resistance. I had finished something.

The manuscript didn't find a publisher and it shouldn't have. It wasn't good enough. I had to go back to a real job, in advertising in New York, and save up again, and quit again, and write another book that also didn't find a publisher because it also wasn't good enough. Neither were the nine screenplays I wrote over the next X years, I can't even remember how many, before I finally got my first check for thirty-five hundred dollars and promptly went back to writing more screenplays that I also couldn't sell.

During that first year, I sometimes thought to myself, "Steve, you've got it lucky now, no distractions, you can focus full-time.

What are you gonna do when life gets complicated again?"

In the end, it didn't matter. That year made me a pro. It gave me, for the first time in my life, an uninterrupted stretch of month after month that was mine alone, that nobody knew about but me, when I was truly productive, truly facing my demons, and truly working my shit.

That year has stuck with me.

THE PAIN OF BEING HUMAN

The Gnostics believed that exile was the essential condition of man. Do you agree? I do.

The artist and the addict both wrestle with this experience of exile. They share an acute, even excruciating sensitivity to the state of separation and isolation, and both actively seek a way to overcome it, to transcend it, or at least to make the pain go away.

What is the pain of being human?

It's the condition of being suspended between two worlds and being unable to fully enter into either.

As mortal flesh, you and I cannot ascend to the upper realm. That sphere belongs to the gods. But we can't put it out of our minds either. We can't escape intimations and half-memories of...what? Some prior sojourn, before birth perhaps, among the immortals or the stars.

Our lot, instead, is to dwell here in the lower realm, the sphere of the temporal and the material—the time-bound dimension of instincts and animal passions, of hate and desire, aspiration and fear.

You and I are called to the upper realm (and it is calling to us), but we're having a pretty good time (sometimes) down here in the sphere of the senses. Bottom line: we're marooned in the middle, stuck inside of Mobile with the Memphis blues again.

JEWISH DESPAIR AND IRISH DESPAIR

If you'll forgive me for quoting myself, here's a passage from *Killing Rommel*.

In the story, a poet and Oxford tutor, Zachary Stein, makes the distinction between two types of despair:

> "Jewish despair arises from want and can be cured by surfeit. Give a penniless Jew fifty quid and he perks right up. Irish despair is different. Nothing relieves Irish despair. The Irishman's complaint lies not with his circumstances, which might be rendered brilliant by labour or luck, but with the injustice of existence itself. Death! How could a benevolent Deity gift us with life, only to set such a cruel term upon it? Irish despair knows no remedy. Money can't help. Love fades. Fame is fleeting. The only cures are booze and sentiment. That's why the Irish are such noble drunks and glorious poets. No one sings like the Irish or mourns like them. Why? Because they're angels imprisoned in vessels of flesh."

It's not just the Irish. The pain of being human is that we're all angels imprisoned in vessels of flesh.

THE PAIN OF BEING HUMAN,
PART TWO

The addict seeks to escape the pain of being human in one of two ways—by transcending it or by anesthetizing it.

Borne aloft by powerful enough chemicals, we can almost, if we're lucky, glimpse the face of the Infinite. If that doesn't work, we can always pass out. Both ways work. The pain goes away.

The artist takes a different tack. She tries to reach the upper realm not by chemicals but by labor and love.

(When I say "artist," I mean as well the lover, the holy man, the engineer, the mother, the warrior, the inventor, the singer, the sage, and the voyager. And remember, addict and artist can be one and the same and often are, moment to moment.)

If the upper realm is, as Plato suggested, the sphere of perfect love, truth, justice, and beauty, then the artist seeks to call down the magic of this world and to create, by dint of labor and luck, the closest-to-sublime simulacra of those qualities that he or she can.

This pursuit produces, for the artist, peace of mind.

BOOK TWO

SELF-INFLICTED WOUNDS

ACCIDENTAL INCAPACITATION

During the trench warfare in WWI, it was a not-uncommon phenomenon for soldiers to take their rifles and literally shoot themselves in the foot. The troopers would claim that the shooting was accidental. They were hoping to get sent to the hospital and thus excused from duty. They did this to avoid the carnage that was waiting for them when the order came to go "over the top," i.e., to mount out of the trenches and charge across no-man's land into the machine-gun fire of the enemy.

In the military, to deliberately inflict injury upon oneself so as to avoid service is called malingering. It's a court-martial offense that is punishable, in some armies, by death.

The habits and addictions of the amateur are conscious or unconscious self-inflicted wounds. Their payoff is incapacity. When we take our M1903 Springfield and blow a hole in our foot, we no longer have to face the real fight of our lives, which is to become who we are and to realize our destiny and our calling.

A DEFINITION OF THE AMATEUR

The amateur is young and dumb. He's innocent, he's good-hearted, he's well-intentioned. The amateur is brave. He's inventive and resourceful. He's willing to take a chance.

Like Luke Skywalker, the amateur harbors noble aspirations. He has dreams. He seeks liberation and enlightenment. And he's willing, he hopes, to pay the price.

The amateur is not evil or crazy. He's not deluded. He's not demented. The amateur is trying to learn.

The amateur is you and me.

What exactly is an amateur? How does an amateur view himself and the world? What qualities characterize the amateur?

THE AMATEUR IS TERRIFIED

Fear is the primary color of the amateur's interior world. Fear of failure, fear of success, fear of looking foolish, fear of under-achieving and fear of over-achieving, fear of poverty, fear of loneliness, fear of death.

But mostly what we all fear as amateurs is being excluded from the tribe, i.e., the gang, the posse, mother and father, family, nation, race, religion.

The amateur fears that if he turns pro and lives out his calling, he will have to live up to who he really is and what he is truly capable of.

The amateur is terrified that if the tribe should discover who he really is, he will be kicked out into the cold to die.

THE PROFESSIONAL
IS TERRIFIED, TOO

The professional, by the way, is just as terrified as the amateur. In fact the professional may be more terrified because she is more acutely conscious of herself and of her interior universe.

The difference—see Part Three—lies in the way the professional acts in the face of fear.

THE AMATEUR IS AN EGOTIST

The amateur identifies with his own ego. He believes he is "himself." That's why he's terrified.

The amateur is a narcissist. He views the world hierarchically. He continuously rates himself in relation to others, becoming self-inflated if his fortunes rise, and desperately anxious if his star should fall.

The amateur sees himself as the hero, not only of his own movie, but of the movies of others. He insists (in his mind, if nowhere else) that others share this view.

The amateur competes with others and believes that he cannot rise unless a competitor falls.

If he had the power, the amateur would eat the world— even knowing that to do so would mean his own extinction.

THE AMATEUR LIVES BY THE OPINIONS OF OTHERS

Though the amateur's identity is seated in his own ego, that ego is so weak that it cannot define itself based on its own self-evaluation. The amateur allows his worth and identity to be defined by others.

The amateur craves third-party validation.

The amateur is tyrannized by his imagined conception of what is expected of him.

He is imprisoned by what he believes he ought to think, how he ought to look, what he ought to do, and who he ought to be.

THE AMATEUR PERMITS FEAR TO
STOP HIM FROM ACTING

Paradoxically, the amateur's self-inflation prevents him from acting. He takes himself and the consequences of his actions so seriously that he paralyzes himself.

The amateur fears, above all else, becoming (and being seen and judged as) himself.

Becoming himself means being different from others and thus, possibly, violating the expectations of the tribe, without whose acceptance and approval, he believes, he cannot survive.

By these means, the amateur remains inauthentic. He remains someone other than who he really is.

THE AMATEUR IS EASILY
DISTRACTED

The amateur has a long list of fears. Near the top are two:

Solitude and silence.

The amateur fears solitude and silence because she needs to avoid, at all costs, the voice inside her head that would point her toward her calling and her destiny. So she seeks distraction.

The amateur prizes shallowness and shuns depth. The culture of Twitter and Facebook is paradise for the amateur.

THE AMATEUR SEEKS INSTANT
GRATIFICATION

There was a popular bumper sticker a few years ago:

Too much ain't enough.

Too much ain't enough, and too soon is too late.

The amateur, the addict and the obsessive all want what they want *now*. The corollary is that, when they get it, it doesn't work. The restlessness doesn't abate, the pain doesn't go away, the fear comes back as soon as the buzz wears off.

THE AMATEUR IS JEALOUS

B ecause the amateur is so powerfully identified with herself, she finds it extremely difficult to view the world through the eyes of others. The amateur is often unkind or insensitive to others, but she saves her most exquisite cruelty for herself.

The amateur's fear eclipses her compassion for others and for herself.

THE AMATEUR LACKS
COMPASSION FOR HIMSELF

In his heart, the amateur knows he's hiding. He knows he was meant for better things. He knows he has turned away from his higher nature.

If the amateur had empathy for himself, he could look in the mirror and not hate what he sees.

Achieving this compassion is the first powerful step toward moving from being an amateur to being a pro.

THE AMATEUR SEEKS PERMISSION

The amateur believes that, before she can act, she must receive permission from some Omnipotent Other—a lover or spouse, a parent, a boss, a figure of authority.

The amateur sits on a stool, like Lana Turner at Schwab's, waiting to be discovered.

THE AMATEUR LIVES FOR THE FUTURE

The amateur and the addict focus exclusively on the product and the payoff. Their concern is what's in it for them, and how soon and how cheaply they can get it.

Consumer culture is designed to exploit the amateur. If you don't believe me, watch ten minutes of TV or scroll through any magazine or online shopping site.

My beef with American culture is that almost every aspect, including the deliberations of the legislature and the judiciary, has been debased to pander to the culture of amateurism. The promise that our products and politicians proffer is the promise one might make to an infant or an addict:

"I will get you what you want and it will cost you nothing."

THE AMATEUR LIVES IN THE PAST

Because the amateur owns nothing of spirit in the present, she either looks forward to a hopeful future or backward to an idyllic past. But the past evoked by the amateur is make-believe. It never existed. It's a highlight reel that she edited together from events that almost took place or should have occurred. In a way, the amateur's re-imagined past is worse when it's true. Because then it's really gone.

The payoff of living in the past or the future is you never have to do your work in the present.

THE AMATEUR WILL BE
READY TOMORROW

Two Hollywood producers were talking. "I've got good news," said one, "and I've got bad news."

"Gimme the good news."

"Remember that mansion we were trying to rent for the big party scene, but we couldn't get because it cost $50K for the night? Well, I just talked to the guy and he'll give it to us for $10K."

"What's the bad news?"

"He wants a hundred bucks up front."

The sure sign of an amateur is he has a million plans and they all start tomorrow.

THE AMATEUR GIVES HIS POWER AWAY TO OTHERS

Have you ever followed a guru or a mentor? I have. I've given my power away to lovers and spouses. I've sat by the phone. I've waited for permission. I've turned in work and awaited, trembling, the judgment of others.

I've given away my power subtly, with a glance that was perceptible to no one. And I've given it away overtly and shamelessly, for all the world to see.

Exile, failure, and banishment can be good things sometimes, because they force us to act from our own center and not from someone else's.

I applaud your story of how you hit bottom, because at the bottom there's no one there but yourself.

THE AMATEUR IS ASLEEP

The force that can save the amateur is awareness, particularly self-awareness. But the amateur understands, however dimly, that if she truly achieved this knowledge, she would be compelled to act upon it.

To act upon this self-awareness would mean defining herself, i.e., differentiating herself from the tribe and thus making herself vulnerable to rejection, expulsion, and all the other fears that self-definition elicits.

Fear of self-definition is what keeps an amateur an amateur and what keeps an addict an addict.

THE TRIBE DOESN'T GIVE A SHIT

The amateur dreads becoming who she really is because she fears that this new person will be judged by others as "different." The tribe will declare us "weird" or "queer" or "crazy." The tribe will reject us.

Here's the truth: the tribe doesn't give a shit.

There is no tribe.

That gang or posse that we imagine is sustaining us by the bonds we share is in fact a conglomeration of individuals who are just as fucked up as we are and just as terrified. Each individual is so caught up in his own bullshit that he doesn't have two seconds to worry about yours or mine, or to reject or diminish us because of it.

When we truly understand that the tribe doesn't give a damn, we're free. There is no tribe, and there never was.

Our lives are entirely up to us.

PART-TIME PROS

Sometimes we can be professionals in our shadow careers but amateurs in our true calling.

How many creative directors at ad agencies have unfinished novels and screenplays sitting in their office drawers? How many lawyers and doctors do you know who would make sensational essayists or novelists or historians but, beyond the odd op-ed submission, never propel themselves past literary first base? I know producers who yearn to be directors, moms who are itching to launch start-ups, grad students who could solve climate change.

Sometimes the reason we choose these careers (consciously or unconsciously) is to produce incapacity.

Resistance is diabolical. It can harness our drive for greatness and our instinct for professionalism and yoke them, instead, to a shadow profession, whose demands will keep us from turning our energies toward their true course.

Sometimes it's easier to be a professional in a shadow career than it is to turn pro in our real calling.

Now, let's talk about turning pro.

LIFE GETS VERY SIMPLE WHEN YOU TURN PRO

What happens when we turn pro is, we finally listen to that still, small voice inside our heads. At last we find the courage to identify the secret dream or love or bliss that we have known all along was our passion, our calling, our destiny.

Ballet.

Motorcycle maintenance.

Founding a clinic in the slums of Sao Paulo.

This, we acknowledge at last, is what we are most afraid of. This is what we know in our hearts we have to do.

HOW YOUR LIFE CHANGES WHEN YOU TURN PRO

I said in *The War of Art* that I could divide my life neatly into two sections: before I turned pro, and after. This is absolutely true.

I didn't change after I turned pro. I did not achieve enlightenment. I'm the same person I always was, with the same weaknesses and the same fallibilities. But everything is different since I turned pro.

Before we turn pro, our life is dominated by fear and Resistance. We live in a state of denial. We're denying the voice in our heads. We're denying our calling. We're denying who we really are.

We're fleeing from our fear into an addiction or a shadow career.

What changes when we turn pro is we stop fleeing.

Be brave, my heart [wrote the poet and mercenary, Archilochus]. *Plant your feet and square your shoulders to the enemy. Meet him among the man-killing spears. Hold your ground.*

When we turn pro, we stop running from our fears. We turn around and face them.

HOW YOUR DAY CHANGES WHEN
YOU TURN PRO

When we turn pro, everything becomes simple. Our aim centers on the ordering of our days in such a way that we overcome the fears that have paralyzed us in the past.

We now structure our hours not to flee from fear, but to confront it and overcome it. We plan our activities in order to accomplish an aim. And we bring our will to bear so that we stick to this resolution.

This changes our days completely.

It changes what time we get up and it changes what time we go to bed. It changes what we do and what we don't do. It changes the activities we engage in and with what attitude we engage in them. It changes what we read and what we eat. It changes the shape of our bodies.

When we were amateurs, our life was about drama, about denial, and about distraction. Our days were simultaneously full to the bursting point and achingly, heartbreakingly empty.

But we are not amateurs any more. We are different, and everyone in our lives sees it.

HOW PEOPLE CHANGE WHEN YOU TURN PRO

Turning pro changes how we spend our time and with whom we spend it.

It changes our friends; it changes our spouses and children. It changes who is drawn to us and who is repelled by us.

Turning pro changes how people perceive us. Those who are still fleeing from their own fears will now try to sabotage us. They will tell us we've changed and try to undermine our efforts at further change. They will attempt to make us feel guilty for these changes. They will try to entice us to get stoned with them or fuck off with them or waste time with them, as we've done in the past, and when we refuse, they will turn against us and talk us down behind our backs.

At the same time, new people will appear in our lives. They will be people who are facing their own fears and who are conquering them. These people will become our new friends.

When we turn pro, we will be compelled to make painful choices. There will be people who in the past had been colleagues and associates, even friends, whom we will no longer be able to spend time with if our intention is to grow and to evolve. We will have to choose between the life we want for our future and the life we have left behind.

HOW YOUR MIND CHANGES WHEN YOU TURN PRO

Turning pro is like kicking a drug habit or stopping drinking. It's a decision, a decision to which we must re-commit every day.

Twelve-step programs say "One Day at a Time." The professional says the same thing.

Each day, the professional understands, he will wake up facing the same demons, the same Resistance, the same self-sabotage, the same tendencies to shadow activities and amateurism that he has always faced.

The difference is that now he will not yield to those temptations.

He will have mastered them, and he will continue to master them.

WHAT MAKES US TURN PRO

Turning pro is a decision. But it's such a monumental, life-overturning decision (and one that is usually made only in the face of overwhelming fear) that the moment is frequently accompanied by powerful drama and emotion. Often it's something we've been avoiding for years, something we would never willingly face unless overwhelming events compelled us to.

Turning pro is like Pearl Harbor or 9/11 or the assassination of President Kennedy. We never forget where we were when it happened.

Here are two turning-pro moments, both from female friends:

MS. X IN BAKERSFIELD

Ms. X is an attorney who lives in Los Angeles. Here's her story:

I was driving, alone, from San Francisco to L.A. I took Interstate 5 because it was faster than the 101 and I had a meeting I had to get to. I got to Bakersfield around five and pulled off to find a gas station.

I woke up the next morning in a motel room, by myself, in the same clothes I had been wearing the night before, with an empty quart of Jim Beam on the bedstand beside me.

Why that time was different from any of a hundred times before, I don't know. But as I was staring at my reflection in the bathroom mirror, I heard my own voice say, "That's enough, darling. This shit has got to stop."

ROSANNE CASH'S DREAM

The following is an excerpt from Rosanne Cash's memoir, *Composed*. Thanks, Rose, for sharing it.
[Note: "King's" in the first sentence refers to *King's Record Shop*, the 1987 album that produced four #1 singles.]

It was late in the making of *King's* that I had a dream that changed my life.

I had met Linda Ronstadt a few times—in Los Angeles, while I was recording at Lania Lane; when I opened for Bonnie Raitt at the Greek Theater and Linda had come to see the show; and on a number of other occasions, as we traveled in the same circles and worked with many of the same musicians. Her record *Heart Like a Wheel* had profoundly affected me as a young girl, and I had studied it assiduously as a great example of a feminine point of view concept record, the best one since Joni Mitchell's *Blue*, I thought, and equally important in the template I was creating for what I might do in my life.

I especially admired her thoughtful song selection, which resulted in a very well-balanced album, and I wanted to make a record with a similarly unified concept, but as a songwriter.

Just as I was beginning to record *King's,* I had read an interview with her in which she said that in committing to artistic growth, you had to "refine your skills to support your instincts." This made such a deep impression on me that I clipped the article to save it. A short time after that, I dreamed I was at a party, sitting on a sofa with Linda and an elderly man who was between us. His name, I somehow knew, was Art. He and Linda were talking animatedly, deeply engrossed in their conversation. I tried to enter the discussion and made a comment to the old man. He turned his head slowly from Linda to me and looked me up and down with obvious disdain and an undisguised lack of interest. "We don't respect dilettantes," he spat out, and turned back to Linda. I felt utterly humiliated and woke from this dream, shaken to the core. I had been growing uneasy in my role in the Nashville community and the music business as a whole. I thought of myself primarily as a songwriter, but I had written only three songs on *King's*. I was famous and successful, but it felt hollow, and the falsehoods were piling up. With more success had come more pressure to be a certain way, to toe a certain line, to start a fan club (which I refused to do), to participate in big, splashy events, and to act as if the country music scene were a religion to which I belonged. I resisted the push to conform, to buy into a certain narrow aesthetic, and to become part of the established hierarchy. I didn't want a lofty perch; I wanted to be in the trenches, where the inspiration was. My unease led me to that dream. Carl Jung said that a person might have five "big" dreams in her life—dreams that provoke a shift in consciousness—and this was my first.

From that moment I changed the way I approached songwriting, I changed how I sang, I changed my work ethic, and I changed my life. The strong desire to become a better songwriter dovetailed perfectly with my budding friendship with John Stewart, who had written "Runaway Train" for *King's Record Shop*. John encouraged me to expand the subject matter in my songs, as well as my choice of language and my mind. I played new songs for him and if he thought it was too "perfect," which was anathema to him, he would say, over and over, "but where's the MADNESS, Rose?" I started looking for the madness. I sought out Marge Rivingston in New York to work on my voice and I started training, as if I were a runner, in both technique and stamina. Oddly, it turned out that Marge also worked with Linda, which I didn't know when I sought her out. I started paying attention to everything, both in the studio and out. If I found myself drifting off into daydreams—an old, entrenched habit—I pulled myself awake and back into the present moment. Instead of toying with ideas, I examined them, and I tested the authenticity of my instincts musically. I stretched my attention span consciously. I read books on writing by Natalie Goldberg and Carolyn Heilbrun and began to self-edit and refine more, and went deeper into every process involved with writing and musicianship. I realized I had earlier been working only within my known range—never pushing far outside the comfort zone to take any real risks...I started painting, so I could learn about the absence of words and sound, and why I needed them. I took painting lessons from Sharon Orr, who had a series of classes at a studio called Art and Soul.

I remained completely humbled by the dream, and it stayed with me through every waking hour of completing *King's Record Shop*...I vowed the next record would reflect my new commitment. Rodney [Crowell, Rosanne's then-husband] was at the top of his game as a record producer, but I had come to feel curiously like a neophyte in the studio after the dream. Everything seemed new, frightening, and tremendously exciting. I had awakened from the morphine sleep of success into the life of an artist.

MY OWN MOMENT OF TURNING PRO

The following is from the chapter called "Resistance and Healing" in *The War of Art:*

I washed up in New York a couple of decades ago, making twenty bucks a night driving a cab and running away full-time from doing my work. One night, alone in my $110-a-month sublet, I hit bottom in terms of having diverted myself into so many phony channels so many times that I couldn't rationalize it for one more evening. I dragged out my ancient Smith-Corona, dreading the experience as pointless, fruitless, meaningless, not to say the most painful exercise I could think of. For two hours I made myself sit there, torturing out some trash that I chucked immediately into the shitcan. That was enough. I put the machine away. I went back to the kitchen. In the sink sat ten days of dishes. For some reason I had enough excess energy that I decided to wash them. The warm water felt pretty good. The soap and sponge were doing their thing. A pile of clean plates began rising in the drying rack. To my amazement I realized that I was whistling.

It hit me that I had turned a corner.

I was okay.

I would be okay from here on.

Do you understand? I hadn't written anything good. It might be years before I would, if I ever did at all. That didn't matter. What counted was that I had, after years of running from it, actually sat down and done my work.

THE NATURE OF EPIPHANIES

We usually think of breakthroughs as ecstatic moments that elevate us from a lower level to a higher. And they do. But there's a paradox. In the moment, an epiphany feels like hell. Like Rosanne Cash's dream, an epiphany trashes us. It exposes us and leaves us naked. We see ourselves plain, and it's not a pretty picture.

The essence of epiphanies is the stripping away of self-delusion. We thought we were X. Now suddenly we see we're minus-X. We're X divided by infinity.

There is great power in this moment.

We've lost something, yes. A cherished self-delusion must be abandoned, and this hurts.

But what we have gained is the truth. Our bullshit falls away. The scales drop from our eyes. In that moment we have two options:

We can reconstitute our bullshit.

Or we can turn pro.

SHAME IS GOOD

In the post-epiphanal moment, we have two things going for us that we didn't have ninety seconds earlier: we have reality and we have humility. These are powerful allies.

And we have a third force working in our favor: shame. Why is shame good? Because shame can produce the final element we need to change our lives: will.

Epiphanies hurt. There's no glory to them. They only make good stories at AA meetings or late at night among other foot soldiers in the trenches.

These soldiers know. Each has his own story, of that ghastly, hideous, excruciating moment when it all turned around for him.

BOOK THREE

THE PROFESSIONAL MINDSET

QUALITIES OF THE PROFESSIONAL

I n *The War of Art*, I listed the following as habits and qualities that the professional possesses that the amateur doesn't:

1. The professional shows up every day

2. The professional stays on the job all day

3. The professional is committed over the long haul

4. For the professional, the stakes are high and real

Further:

5. The professional is patient

6. The professional seeks order

7. The professional demystifies

8. The professional acts in the face of fear

9. The professional accepts no excuses

10. The professional plays it as it lays

11. The professional is prepared

12. The professional does not show off

13. The professional dedicates himself to mastering technique

14. The professional does not hesitate to ask for help

15. The professional does not take failure or success personally

16. The professional does not identify with his or her instrument

17. The professional endures adversity

18. The professional self-validates

19. The professional reinvents herself

20. The professional is recognized by other professionals

Here are a few additional qualities, before we move on to the higher expression of professionalism:

A PROFESSIONAL IS COURAGEOUS

The professional displays courage, not only in the roles she embraces (which invariably scare the hell out of her) or the sacrifices she makes (of time, love, family) or even in the enduring of criticism, blame, envy, and lack of understanding, but above all in the confronting of her own doubts and demons.

The linebacker and the Army Ranger go into action as part of a team. But the artist and the entrepreneur enter combat alone. I take my hat off to every man or woman who does this.

THE PROFESSIONAL
WILL NOT BE DISTRACTED

The amateur tweets. The pro works.

THE PROFESSIONAL IS RUTHLESS
WITH HIMSELF

Picasso was in his Paris studio (a true story) with the owner of the gallery where his paintings were displayed and sold. The Spaniard was showing off his latest series of portraits, which he had labored for months to produce. The gallery owner was ecstatic. He couldn't wait to get these brilliant new works into the gallery and start selling them.

Suddenly Picasso seized a palette knife and strode to the first painting. To the gallery owner's horror, Picasso slashed the canvas from end to end.

"Pablo! *Arret*, Pablito!"

But Picasso didn't stop. Blade in hand, he marched down the line of paintings, reducing each one to ribbons.

The professional knows when he has fallen short of his own standards. He will murder his darlings without hesitation, if that's what it takes to stay true to the goddess and to his own expectations of excellence.

THE PROFESSIONAL HAS COMPASSION FOR HERSELF

I got the chance a few years ago to watch a famous trainer work with his thoroughbreds. I had imagined that the process would be something hard-core like Navy SEAL training. To my surprise, the sessions were more like play.

The work was serious, as in teaching the two-year-olds to enter the starting gate, and the horses were definitely learning. But the trainer took pains to make the schooling feel like fun. When a horse got tired, the trainer took him off the track. If a mount got bored or restive, the trainer never forced him to continue or drove him "through the pain."

He explained:

> A horse is a flight animal. Even a stallion, if he can, will choose flight over confrontation. Picture the most sensitive person you've ever known; a horse is ten times more sensitive. A horse is a naked nervous system, particularly a thoroughbred. He's a child. A three-year-old, big and fast as he is, is a baby. Horses understand the whip, but I don't want a racer that runs that way. A horse that loves to run will beat a horse that's compelled, every day of the week.

I want my horses to love the track. I want
my exercise riders to have to hold them
back in the morning because they're so
excited to get out and run.

Never train your horse to exhaustion.
Leave him wanting more.

THE PROFESSIONAL LIVES
IN THE PRESENT

The amateur spends his time in the past and the future. He permits himself to fear and to hope.

The professional has taught himself to banish these distractions.

When Stephen Sondheim makes a hat, he is thinking of nothing else. He is immersed. He loses himself in the work and in the moment.

THE PROFESSIONAL DEFERS
GRATIFICATION

I'm guilty of checking my e-mail. Are you?

We're crazy.

What do we imagine we're going to find in our Inbox?

The children who were able to sit for three minutes with a marshmallow on the table in front of them without eating it were rewarded with two marshmallows when the experimenter returned.

But that's as crazy as inbox-watching.

Krishna said we have the right to our labor, but not to the fruits of our labor. He meant that the piano is its own reward, as is the canvas, the barre, and the movieola.

Fuck the marshmallows.

THE PROFESSIONAL DOES NOT
WAIT FOR INSPIRATION

W e're all nothing without the Muse. But the pro has learned that the goddess prizes labor and dedication beyond any theatrical seeking of her favors. The professional does not wait for inspiration; he acts in anticipation of it.

He knows that when the Muse sees his butt in the chair, she will deliver.

THE PROFESSIONAL DOES NOT
GIVE HIS POWER AWAY TO OTHERS

The dictionary defines "icon" as an article (a relic, say, that once belonged to a saint or a holy man) that serves as an object of worship.

A person can be an icon.

When we make someone into an icon, we give away our power. We say to ourselves (unconsciously), "This person possesses qualities I wish I possessed. Therefore I will worship this person in the hope that that quality will wear off on me, or I will acquire that quality by virtue of my proximity to this mentor/sensei/lover/teacher/hero."

In my experience, when we project a quality or virtue onto another human being, we ourselves almost always already possess that quality, but we're afraid to embrace (and to live) that truth.

The amateur is an acolyte, a groupie. The professional may seek instruction or wisdom from one who is further along in mastery than he, but he does so without surrendering his self-sovereignty.

THE PROFESSIONAL HELPS OTHERS

When I first finished the manuscript for *Gates of Fire*, it was 800 pages long. My agent, Sterling Lord, though he loved it, said it couldn't submit it to publishers unless I cut at least 300 pages. That was like telling me to amputate not one limb, but two. I was devastated.

One of the people Sterling had shown the manuscript to was Tom Guinzburg, who had been head of Viking Press for years. It was a helluva thing for someone of Tom's stature simply to glance at an unknown writer's work. But Tom did more. He sent me a note. I still have it. The central sentence said:

> There's something great in here, Steve.
> I have confidence that you will find it and
> bring it out.

I barely knew Tom, and he barely knew me. But if you saw the thumbprints I put on that note, from the dozens of times I picked it up and hung onto its words for inspiration, you would think we were the best of buds from way back.

The amateur hoards his knowledge and his reinforcement. He believes that if he shares what he possesses with others, he will lose it.

The professional is happy to teach. He will gladly lend a hand or deliver a swift kick. But there's a caveat.

The professional refuses to be iconized. Not for selfish reasons, but because he knows how destructive the dynamic of iconization is to the iconizer. The pro will share his wisdom with other professionals—or with amateurs who are committed to becoming professionals.

Like "Art" in Rosanne Cash's dream, he will not waste his time on dilettantes.

WHAT ABOUT THE MAGIC?

The professional mindset works in two ways. It's important for us to grasp the distinction.

First, the pro mindset is a discipline that we use to overcome Resistance. To defeat the self-sabotaging habits of procrastination, self-doubt, susceptibility to distraction, perfectionism, and shallowness, we enlist the self-strengthening habits of order, regularity, discipline, and a constant striving after excellence. That's not hard to understand.

But what about the magic? What about madness? What about flashes of brilliance and uncontrollable outbursts of genius? How does the professional mindset help there? Isn't it too severe, too hardcore, too regimented?

Answer: no.

The monk glimpses the face of God not by scaling a peak in the Himalayas, but by sitting still in silence.

Yoga, meditation, and the martial arts access the soul by way of the body. The physical leads to the spiritual. The humble produces the sublime.

It seems counterintuitive, but it's true: in order to achieve "flow," magic, "the zone," we start by being common and ordinary and workmanlike. We set our palms against the stones in the garden wall and search, search, search until at last, in the instant when we're ready to give up, our fingers fasten upon the secret door.

Like a child entering a meadow, we step over the threshold, forgetting everything except the butterfly that flits across our vision.

From this play arises *Guernica* and *The Godfather* and the Guggenheim Museum Bilbao.

A MARINE GETS TWO SALARIES

There's a well-known gunnery sergeant who, when his young Marines complain about their pay, explains that they get two salaries:

A financial salary and a psychological salary.

The Marine's financial salary is indeed meager. But what about the psychological salary—the feeling of pride and honor, the sense of belonging to a brotherhood with a brave and noble history, and knowing that, no matter what happens, you remain a member of that fraternity as long as you live? How much, the Gunny asks, is that worth?

You and I, as artists and entrepreneurs, receive two salaries as well.

The first might be called conventional rewards—money, applause, attention. That kind is fine, if we can get it. The problem for most of us is we can't. We bust our butts training and practicing and studying and rehearsing and nobody shows up, nobody notices, nobody even knows we exist. No wonder people quit. The struggle requires too much agony for too little payoff.

That's the conventional reward.

Then there's the psychological reward.

Remember, Krishna told Arjuna that he had the right to his labor, but not to the fruits of his labor. What he meant was conventional fruits. Does the monk meditate only to achieve enlightenment? What if that never happens?

What does the dancer take from ballet class? Is it fun for the actor to perform? Why does the singer sing or the filmmaker shoot?

When we do the work for itself alone (I know how easy that is to say and how hard it is to do), we're like that Marine who sleeps in a foxhole in the freezing rain but who knows a secret that only he and his brothers and sisters share.

When we do the work for itself alone, our pursuit of a career (or a living or fame or wealth or notoriety) turns into something else, something loftier and nobler, which we may never even have thought about or aspired to at the beginning.

It turns into a practice.

MY YEARS IN THE WILDERNESS

In a way I was lucky that I experienced failure for so many years. Because there were no conventional rewards, I was forced to ask myself, Why am I doing this? Am I crazy? All my friends are making money and settling down and living normal lives. What the hell am I doing? Am I nuts? What's wrong with me?

In the end I answered the question by realizing that I had no choice. I couldn't do anything else. When I tried, I got so depressed I couldn't stand it. So when I wrote yet another novel or screenplay that I couldn't sell, I had no choice but to write another after that. The truth was, I was enjoying myself. Maybe nobody else liked the stuff I was doing, but I did. I was learning. I was getting better.

The work became, in its own demented way, a practice. It sustained me, and it sustains me still.

THE PROFESSIONAL MINDSET
AS A PRACTICE

What is a practice anyway?

To "have a practice" in yoga, say, or tai chi, or calligraphy, is to follow a rigorous, prescribed regimen with the intention of elevating the mind and the spirit to a higher level.

A practice implies engagement in a ritual. A practice may be defined as the dedicated, daily exercise of commitment, will, and focused intention aimed, on one level, at the achievement of mastery in a field but, on a loftier level, intended to produce a communion with a power greater than ourselves—call it whatever you like: God, mind, soul, Self, the Muse, the superconscious.

The following are aspects of any practice:

A PRACTICE HAS A SPACE

A practice has a space, and that space is sacred.

There's a wonderful book called *Where Women Create*. It's a compilation of photos of studios and workshops where various female artists do their magic. The workspaces are those of potters and weavers, quilters and dressmakers, architects and sculptors, painters, filmmakers, editors. The book has an excellent text, but you don't need to read it. Just look at these sacred spaces. What you'll see is this:

> Order
>
> Commitment
>
> Passion
>
> Love
>
> Intensity
>
> Beauty
>
> Humility

Twenty-six artists with twenty-six different personal odysseys. Many, no doubt, include divorce, heartbreak, alcoholism, you name it. But every woman in this book has, in her artistic life, transcended these impediments, and every one has arrived at the same space.

They all serve the Muse. And each has discovered in that service her unique and authentic essence.

A PRACTICE HAS A TIME

The monks in their saffron robes mount the steps to the zendo at the same hour each morning. When the abbot strikes the chime, the monks place their palms together and sit.

You and I may have to operate in a more chaotic universe. But the object remains the same: to approach the mystery via order, commitment and passionate intention.

When we convene day upon day in the same space at the same time, a powerful energy builds up around us. This is the energy of our intention, of our dedication, of our commitment.

The goddess sees this energy and she rewards it.

A PRACTICE HAS AN INTENTION

When Stevie Wonder sits down in his studio at the piano, he's not there to mess around.

Stevie has come to work.

The 10,000 Hour Rule, made famous by Malcolm Gladwell in his book, *Outliers,* postulates that the achievement of mastery in any field, be it brain surgery or throwing a split-finger fastball, requires approximately 10,000 hours of practice. But the key, according to Mr. Gladwell, is that that practice be focused.

It must possess intention.

Our intention as artists is to get better, to go deeper, to work closer and closer to the bone.

WE COME TO A PRACTICE AS WARRIORS

The sword master stepping onto the fighting floor knows he will be facing powerful opponents. Not the physical adversaries whom he will fight (though those indeed serve as stand-ins for the enemy). The real enemy is inside himself.

The monk in meditation knows this. So does the yogi. So do the film editor and the video-game creator and the software writer.

Each day we, as professionals, face the same monsters and chimeras as did Perseus or Bellerophon or St. George.

The sword master advancing into ritual combat has inwardly made peace with his own extinction. He is prepared to leave everything, including his life, there on the fighting floor.

WE COME TO A PRACTICE IN HUMILITY

We may bring intention and intensity to our practice (in fact we must), but not ego. Dedication, even ferocity, yes. But never arrogance.

The space of the practice is sacred. It belongs to the goddess. We take our shoes off before we enter. We press our palms together and we bow.

Do you understand how the mystery can be approached via order?

WE COME TO A PRACTICE AS STUDENTS

Even the peerless sword master Miyamoto Musashi entered the fighting square to learn as much as to teach.

A PRACTICE IS LIFELONG

The Spartan king Agesilaus was still fighting in armor when he was eighty-two. Picasso was painting past ninety, and Henry Miller was chasing women (I'm sure Picasso was too) at eighty-nine.

Once we turn pro, we're like sharks who have tasted blood, or renunciants who have glimpsed the face of God. For us, there is no finish line. No bell ends the bout. Life is the pursuit. Life is the hunt. When our hearts burst...then we'll go out, and no sooner.

ROSANNE CASH'S DREAM, PART TWO

The specific details of acquiring professionalism evolve naturally. They're self-evident. When Rosanne Cash had her dream, she got the message.

The epiphany is everything. When we see the gaping holes in our practice (or discover that we have no practice at all), no one has to school us in time management or resource allocation.

We know what we have to do.

The other thing about the changes Rosanne made after her dream is that she didn't make those changes to earn more money, or achieve greater fame, or to sell more records. She made those changes out of respect for her craft. She made them to become a better artist and a more powerful musician.

When we raise our game aesthetically, we elevate it morally and spiritually as well.

THE PROFESSIONAL TRUSTS
THE MYSTERY

P atricia Ryan Madson taught improv at Stanford for years to standing-room-only classes. (Her book *Improv Wisdom* is on my short list of indispensables.) Patricia has an exercise that she calls "What's in the Box?"

She asks her students to imagine a small white box. Imagine a lid on this box. Now lift the lid.

What do you find inside?

Sometimes students say a diamond. Sometimes a frog. Sometimes a pomegranate.

The trick is, there is always *something* inside the box.

With this exercise, Patricia was addressing her students' seminal terror: that they would get up on stage and draw a blank.

The professional trusts the mystery. He knows that the Muse always delivers. She may surprise us. She may give us something we never expected.

But she will always put something inside the box.

The following are five axioms, derived from this principle, that I work by every day:

WORK OVER YOUR HEAD

Writers of fiction learn early that it is possible to write a character who is smarter than they are.

How can that be?

The answer lies in the Mystery.

That place that we write from (or paint from or compose from or innovate from) is far deeper than our petty personal egos. That place is beyond intellect. It is deeper than rational thought.

It is instinct.

It is intuition.

It is imagination.

If you and I cast Meryl Streep as Queen Boudica in our next Hollywood blockbuster, will we have any doubts that she can pull it off (even though she has never heard of, and knows nothing about, Queen Boudica)?

Ms. Streep will go wherever it is that she goes, and she'll come back with Queen Boudica. She will have become Queen Boudica.

You and I can do it, too. We can work over our heads. Not only can we, but we must.

The best pages I've ever written are pages I can't remember writing.

WRITE WHAT YOU DON'T KNOW

Years ago, in New York, I had hit the wall as a failed novelist. My next day's to-do list had been reduced to two options:

Kill myself by hanging.

Kill myself by jumping off the roof.

Instead I decided to write a screenplay.

The story I wrote was about prison. I have never been to prison. I didn't know the first thing about prison. But I was so desperate that I plunged in, slinging bullshit with both hands and not looking back. When I was done, I showed the script to a few writers I knew.

More than one tugged me aside and asked in a whisper, "Steve, where did you do time?"

Good things happen when we trust the Mystery.

There is always something in the box.

TAKE WHAT THE DEFENSE
GIVES YOU

E very book I write has at least one giant section that's as tough as a knot in a plank of lumber. I can't crack it head-on. Attacking from the flank doesn't work. The damn thing is just too stubborn.

When you're up against that kind of Resistance, there's no shame in taking what the defense will give you. In football terms, we shut that part of the playbook that contains the deep "go" routes and the 55-yard bombs. We turn instead to that section that has the short slants and the three-yard dinks into the flat.

Two key tenets for days when Resistance is really strong:

1. Take what you can get and stay patient.
    The defense may crack late in the game.

2. Play for tomorrow.

Our role on tough-nut days is to maintain our composure and keep chipping away. We're pros. We're not amateurs. We have patience. We can handle adversity.

Tomorrow the defense will give us more, and tomorrow we'll take it.

There's a third tenet that underlies the first two:

3. We're in this for the long haul.

Our work is a practice. One bad day is nothing to us. Ten bad days are nothing.

In the scheme of our lifelong practice, twenty-four hours when we can't gain yardage is only a speed bump. We'll forget it by breakfast tomorrow and be back again, ready to hurl our bodies into the fray.

PLAY HURT

The amateur believes that she must have all her ducks in a row before she can launch her start-up or compose her symphony or design her iPhone app.

The professional knows better.

Has your husband just walked out on you? Has your El Dorado been repossessed?

Keep writing.

Keep composing.

Keep shooting film.

Athletes play hurt. Warriors fight scared.

The professional takes two aspirin and keeps on truckin'.

SIT CHILLY

Sue Sally Hale was a famous equestrienne and teacher of horsemanship. She had a phrase that she drilled into her students' heads:

"Sit chilly."

If you and I are riding in a steeplechase, we may find ourselves at the gallop atop our thousand-pound or twelve-hundred-pound hunter-jumper, approaching a stone wall that looks like it's fifteen feet high. Dire thoughts may enter our heads at that moment.

Trickier still, the rider's "seat"—meaning the way we sit in the saddle—is how our intentions are communicated to the ultra-sensitive mount beneath us. If fear and uncertainty enter our minds, our horse will know instantly. At that point, anything can happen.

Sue Sally said, "Sit chilly."

She meant not just "be cool" or "stay composed." She meant maintain your seat.

The professional knows that, in the course of her pursuit, she will inevitably experience moments of terror, even panic. She knows she can't choke that panic back or wish it away. It's there, and it's for real.

The pro sits chilly.

She focuses on the horse and the wall. She keeps her seat.

THE PROFESSIONAL AND THE
PRIMITIVE

A couple of years ago I got the chance to travel to Africa. Among the places I visited was a Masai camp. The site was so far out in the boonies that we had to fly to it. There were no roads. We had two city Masai with us, a young man and a young woman, who did the translating.

When we landed, a commotion was going on. Our guides explained to us, after speaking with several of the camp elders, that the shaman had just determined that the place where the village had set up camp was "unwholesome." So everyone was packing up to move.

The population of the camp was about five hundred—warriors, kids, old folks, plus all the tribe's livestock. The ceremony of moving camp required that the procession be led by the white cattle, so these were being rounded up. This was no simple operation, as the individual cows were owned by different families and were scattered all over the valley. We watched for more than an hour while the elders, under the direction of the shaman, collected the white cattle and herded them to the front of the procession. The whole tribe had packed up now. The warriors—the tall, slim *morans*—were singing a ritual song and jumping up and down, surrounded by the pretty young maidens, contributing their own chorus.

Finally the village moved.

About two hundred yards up the hill.

"That's it?" one of the visitors asked.

We were watching the shaman. Yep, that was it. He had solved the problem. The new campsite was much better.

At the time I didn't think much about this. It all seemed perfectly natural and in keeping with Africa and tribal life. But when I got home, I began to wonder about the assumptions, as imperfectly as I could grasp them, that underpinned this whole extravaganza:

1. Some invisible force threatened the first camp. Ghosts? Restive ancestors? Free-floating evil? Would wicked things befall the tribespeople if they remained in the first camp?

2. This invisible evil could be warded off by moving the camp—even though that move was only a few hundred feet. How did that make sense? Couldn't the evil force simply follow the tribe up the hill and work its malice in the new camp? Why did such a simple fix solve the problem?

3. One individual, the shaman, was capable of perceiving this evil force, of divining its malign intent, and of remedying this by a specific course of action.

4. The tribe followed the shaman's instructions without a murmur of protest. No matriarch complained about having to pack up her stuff, which for each family was considerable and which involved a serious amount of labor and sweat. No warrior resisted. One and all, the people fell into line and participated freely and cheerfully.

(I must observe, of myself, that I too accepted the shaman's wisdom. When we got uphill to the new camp, I confess, it felt better. I was glad we had moved.)

5. Lastly, I considered the Masai culture itself. These were no benighted primitives being exploited by some canny hoo-doo man. The Masai were and are one of the great warrior cultures of all time. They have been in East Africa since the 1500s (longer than the existence of the U.S. of A.) and they've thrived and dominated in a harsh land peopled by proud, strong, and aggressive adversaries.

Beyond that, the culture of the Masai is brilliant—their dress, their rituals, their social organization. They are tall, strong, and beautiful. Their young men stand up to lions single-handedly and slay the beasts with only a spear. They must be doing something right.

What if, I asked myself, the Masai view of the world is correct? What if there really was an evil force threatening the lower camp? What if the shaman really saw it and concocted exactly the right remedy? Maybe if we had stayed in the lower camp, one of the pregnant young wives would have miscarried. Maybe a fight would have broken out between two braves and one of them would have hurt the other. Maybe the whole village would have been seized by collective evil.

What does all this have to do with the professional and the idea of turning pro?

Here's what I think:

My worldview is pretty much that of the Masai. I believe in the shaman. I wish I had a shaman. If I had a shaman, I would have breakfast with him every morning, and whatever he told me to do that day, I would do it.

Better yet, I wish I was a shaman.

In truth, I practice my own form of shamanism every day. As an artist, I seek to access unseen powers. Evil forces are out there—Resistance, self-doubt, self-sabotage. How many other malign entities are hovering each morning over me and my huevos rancheros?

Then there are the good forces. Inspiration, enthusiasm, courage. New ideas, brilliant breakthroughs, insights, intuitions. Where do these come from? I don't know. How can I access them? I have no clue.

Yet this is my business. This is my life.

Damn right I want that shaman. He is my man! I love the guy!

In lieu of the shaman, I have...what?

I have a code of professionalism. I have virtues that I seek to strengthen and vices that I labor to eradicate.

I serve the goddess. Where she tells me to go, I go.

I wish I knew that shaman. I would love to sit down with him. I'd ask him what he saw that morning. How did he see it? What course of initiation had he undergone to acquire his knowledge?

Does he serve the gods like I do? Does he regard his gifts as a blessing or a curse?

A MODEL OF THE UNIVERSE

I was having breakfast with my friend Rabbi Mordecai Finley of Ohr HaTorah congregation in Los Angeles. I wanted to ask him about the subject of Resistance. Is there a parallel in Kabbalistic studies or Jewish mysticism? Here's part (I tape-recorded it) of what he said:

> "There is a second self inside you—
> an inner, shadow Self. This self doesn't
> care about you. It doesn't love you. It
> has its own agenda, and it will kill you.
> It will kill you like cancer. It will kill
> you to achieve its agenda, which is to
> prevent you from actualizing your Self,
> from becoming who you really are.
> This shadow self is called, in the
> Kabbalistic lexicon, the *yetzer hara*. The
> yetzer hara, Steve, is what you would
> call Resistance."

In the Kabbalistic view of the world, the soul (*neshama* in Hebrew) is the source of all wisdom and goodness. The neshama seeks constantly to communicate to us—to our consciousness on the physical plane. The soul is trying to guide us, sustain us, restore us.

But there is a force operating in opposition to the neshama. This entity, the yetzer hara, is a self-sustaining and cunning intelligence whose sole aim is to block us from accessing the neshama and to block the neshama from communicating to us.

The Gnostics and the neo-Platonists believed something very much like this. In both models of the universe, there was an upper realm (in Plato's conception, the realm of the Forms—of perfect beauty, justice, truth, and so forth) and a lower sphere where we mortals dwelt.

In Jewish mysticism, there is a positive force that opposes the yetzer hara. Above every blade of grass, says the Kabbalah, hovers an angel, exhorting "Grow! Grow!"

What program did these ancients put forward as a means of allying with the positive forces and overcoming the negative? According to Rabbi Finley, it was a code called Mussar.

MUSSAR

M ussar (pronounced moo-SAHR) was a code of ethical discipline. It was not far from what we see today in twelve-step programs.

Its first tenet was "identify the sin." The second was "eliminate it."

In AA terms, this would mean:

> 1. Acknowledge the condition of
>   being an alcoholic
>
> 2. Stop drinking

The Kabbalists believed that the higher realm could be approached through a disciplined, humble, and open application of the mind and will. They recognized that they were approaching a mystery. They knew that an enemy was seeking to block them.

What they called mussar, I call turning pro.

Our job, as souls on this mortal journey, is to shift the seat of our identity from the lower realm to the upper, from the ego to the Self.

Art (or, more exactly, the struggle to produce art) teaches us that.

When you and I struggle against Resistance (or seek to love or endure or give or sacrifice), we are engaged in a contest not only on the material, mental, and emotional planes, but on the spiritual as well. The struggle is not only to write our symphony or to raise our child or to lead our Special Forces team against the Taliban in Konar province. The clash is epic and internal, between the ego and the Self, and the stakes are our lives.

WHO IS ALL THIS FOR?

In the end, the enterprise and the sacrifice are all about the audience.

They're about the readers, the moviegoers, the site visitors, the listeners, the concertgoers, the gamers, the gallery-goers—a group which, by the way, includes you and me.

We're the audience.

In the hero's journey, the wanderer returns home after years of exile, struggle, and suffering. He brings a gift for the people. That gift arises from what the hero has seen, what he has endured, what he has learned. But the gift is not that raw material alone. It is the ore refined into gold by the hero/wanderer/artist's skilled and loving hands.

You are that artist.

I will gladly shell out $24.95 or $9.99 or 99 cents on iTunes to read or see or listen to the 24-karat treasure that you have refined from your pain and your vision and your imagination. I need it. We all do. We're struggling here in the trenches. That beauty, that wisdom, those thrills and chills, even that mindless escape on a rainy October afternoon—I want it. Put me down for it.

The hero wanders. The hero suffers. The hero returns.

You are that hero.

STEVEN PRESSFIELD is the author of *Gates of Fire, Tides of War, The Afghan Campaign, The Profession, The Warrior Ethos* and *The War of Art,* among others. He lives in Los Angeles. In 2008, he was made an honorary citizen by the city of Sparta in Greece.

36920106R00091

Made in the USA
San Bernardino, CA
05 August 2016